10 Lessons to Escape Mediocrity and Build Your Dreams.

By: Maxamillian Alexander Dutton

Preface.

My name is Maxamillian Alexander Dutton and I'm a United States Marine, Recruiter, Sales Trainer, Mindset Coach and Motivational Speaker. For the last decade I've studied the art of building a winning mindset dedicated to personal success. I find that an individual's mindset can be their greatest asset or their greatest liability. Which is why I've created a dedicated coaching program to help people escape the mundane nature of life and ultimately reach their personal and professional goals.

People want to be able to build the life of their dreams. They want the respect, ability to provide value and a beautiful lifestyle but oftentimes they are missing the foundation of this monumental structure they are trying to create. The foundation of which I speak is your mindset. Your thoughts can have crushing ramifications on any goal that you want to achieve. When we allow doubt to creep into our minds we open the door for mediocrity. I'm sure there's someone out there who wants to live a mediocre lifestyle but I would imagine for most of us, there's more to our story than that.

The purpose of my life is to help people discover the power and potential they have, teach them the art of selling their valuable products and services and create a winning mindset that can achieve anything. My self discovery came from hardship and struggle which allowed me to recognize it. Many people are not that lucky.

There's never a shortage of people trying to escape the 9 to 5 headlock. When I look at the people of this century, I see a group of motivated and eager individuals who want to achieve something but for some reason can't find their footing. If it's your vision to create a business, start a hobby or follow a dream, this book is for you.

In order to build a successful business or have a successful life you need to first build a mindset designed for success. This book is the first of a series of books that will take you from whatever position you are currently in, to a mentally strong motivator capable of achieving whatever goals you have set for yourself.

If you find value in this book, please join me on social media and allow me to share my message with you everyday. You will join a tribe of winners who are focused on growth, providing value and living this one life to the fullest.

Visit Duttonmindset.com to learn more.

Without further ado I present:

10 Lessons to Escape Mediocrity and Build Your Dreams

For you.

LESSON 1: WHO ARE YOU?

The question is: Who are you? I mean really. Who are you? We wake up every single day and we wonder what the purpose of life is. Where do we go? What do we do? We're going to work, we're earning a paycheck, we're coming home, watching TV, we're hanging out with our families, we go to sleep, we wake up, we do it again. Who are you? Is that who you are?

Are you a person that wakes up and works for someone else? Do you exist for someone else? Are you the person that gets paid, spends their money on nothing but bills? Who are you? The person that wakes up every single day, more tired than yesterday, is that you? Are you the person that lives for the weekend? Are you the person that's following someone else's dream? Are you the person who is alone in your thoughts? Are you the person whose mind drifts wishing things were just a little different?

Wishing you had the next promotion? Wishing you could make a little bit more? Wishing you could be in better shape? Wishing you had a little bit more discipline in your life to figure out who you were meant to be? The discipline to figure out how to get what you want?

We all struggle with this idea of who we are in this world. You have the main characters and you have non-player characters. We all think we are the main character. We all want to be a main character, so in our mind we are the main character. We grow up with the idea that we're supposed to be our own main character, yet we live the life of the non-player character and don't realize it. We live a life for others. We try to be others, we try to live like others, we try to act like others, we try to dress like others. Who are you?

What value have you created in this world today? What things have you done for your community today? Where do you fall on the spectrum between non-player characters versus main characters? The main characters make changes. The main characters own their life. The main characters change the world around them to fit their needs. Who are you?

It's got to be tiring thinking you're the main character when really you're a fraud. There's nothing wrong with just being alive right? Everyone needs to be respected. Everyone needs to feel appreciated. Is that all there is to life? Is that all there is for you? Creation used to be easier. Creativity used to be mandatory. You weren't standing out unless you were original. But now there's no such thing as originality. Now everybody's the same. On social media everyone uses the same filters the same way. The same TikToks. People don't even use their own voice. They use the voice of the creator. Who was the creator?

Devices are being made by the master to live a life inside of a dream. Meta. Is it because life outside of the Meta isn't satisfactory? Is it because you can enjoy your life the way you can't in reality? You're able to live the life that you want in a fictional world. To be who you want in a fictional world. To date who you want in a fictional world. Buy what you want in a fictional world. Is it because you cannot create value in the world in which you live in today as it sits right now? You are incapable of making the change. But that doesn't mean you don't want to. You just don't know how to. People sell you a quick fix. That's what they want you to think. To think there's a special secret sauce. A special thing made just for you. Some type of special ingredient that's going to take you from zero to hero. And while you sit in a room and pretend, they make millions off the backs of people just like you. I have fallen victim to scams just like these. People overcharge for products that do nothing. Nothing more than a snake in sheep's clothing. There is a vision that I have, that I can take people and help them find their own reality. To live life. The escape from the grip of social norms.

People are capable of such amazing things in life. So much intelligence wasted. So much potential wasted. So many opportunities to grow. So many opportunities to add value. So many opportunities to add a change. So many opportunities to make a difference.

People's beliefs today are often not even their own. Everything is politicized. The health system is politicized. The school system is politicized. Social media is politicized. The great divide infects our community from things that don't exist, from powers that cannot be seen. This system is not run by one entity but a collection of energy from the individual fighting against one another. Right versus wrong. Or is it wrong versus right?

The chain starts with the individual. I grew up in a world that was designed to make me an absolute failure. I grew up with drug addicted parents and abusive family dynamics. I grew up in poverty. I grew up in a world where there was no plumbing, and we were in the United States of America. Shitting in a bucket like an animal and throwing it out the window. I grew up in a world where sex was introduced young. I grew up in a world where it wasn't weird to do drugs as a kid. I grew up in a world where it wasn't weird to get drunk and stumble home as a kid. I grew up in a world where it didn't seem like there was a choice. I grew up in an environment where the choice was made for you. I grew up in an environment that allowed me to have an excuse.

This is not a book about my life. It's not a book about where I come from. It's not a book about my struggles. This is simply a book that was written to let you know that you do have a choice despite your environment. You do not have to be a product of it. You have a choice. It doesn't matter where you grew up, who your parents were or where you were

raised. Every person knows the difference
between right and wrong. Good and bad.
We decide as to what we want to do with
that life. We make a choice as to what road
we want to embark on.

My question for you remains the same.
Who are you? Who are you? My reader,
who are you? Have you determined what
you want in this world? Have you found a
way to get it? Have you found a way to
add value? Are you OK with rejection? Are
you OK with failure? Because to succeed
you must be OK with that. Success doesn't
mean that you are known around the
world. Success doesn't mean that you are a
millionaire. Success doesn't mean that you
can buy every expensive thing you want in
this world. Success simply means that you

know who you are and that you do what you do because it creates value for the people around you and helps you enjoy the life that you live. In your way, in your world, you can make the change you want to see. You can be the change you want to see. Whatever comes with that comes with it. Everyone can't be famous. If we are all famous then no one is famous.

What about finding your inner strength? It's about finding your inner will to make the decision to be you. It's about developing drive. It's about developing a Mindset. Mindset is a beautiful thing because it's just like a light switch. You have the absolute control to change your entire environment, your entire world, your entire life, your entire existence with the flick of a switch.

If you're sad, you can make yourself happy. If you're tired, you can wake yourself up. If you're fat you can make the choice to get up and walk. You can be anything that you want in this world, you just have to stop waiting for the acceptance of everyone around you.

The only acceptance that matters is from within. Not your social media followers. Not your parents, wife, husband or the Church. You make the change and the decision to do what needs to be done for you. So again, my question remains the same. Who are you?

I hope this book helps take you from that non-player character mindset, the individual that is simply designed to just exist, to the person who is the main character. The person who chooses their own destiny. Who's not afraid to go against the current. Who is not afraid to go against the crowd. The person who is willing and able to do anything at any time. Willing to do whatever it takes to achieve his or her dream.

I hope this book helps you with a mindset that can be just like that light switch. Flip. I truly believe if I can do it anyone can do it. At what point are you going to determine that enough is enough. At what point are you going to step up to the plate and live? It's time to make the desired change.

LESSON 2: THE FINALITY OF LIFE.

This life is crazy because you never know if you're going to live or if you're going to die. You don't know. You could be alive today walking down the street and get hit by a car. A random event to say the least. You had no idea it was going to happen and just like that, you're dead. It is just as fast as the blink of an eye. Just as fast as you were born to this world you were taken out of it. I can only imagine that you probably wouldn't even feel it. You'd have no idea that it even happened.

The people around you were the ones who suffered that loss. Some suffer the loss because they had so many things they have yet to say. Many of them suffer the loss because they had never experienced someone close to them die before. That takes an emotional toll.

Life is finite. There is an ending. I don't care what anyone says, I don't care how spiritual you are and I don't care what you believe in. No one in the existence of this Earth has ever been able to prove that you get to have more than one life. Once it's over, it's over. There's no going back.

So what's the question you're going to have in your mind when it is your time? Let's assume that your death is not as fortunate as our example. Let's assume that it's a slow one. You get the news. You're not going to be able to live another year. Let's assume that a doctor told you your time is almost up. It's at this moment you have to ask yourself, "Am I happy with what I've done? Have I left my mark?" Did you ever want to leave a mark? Was it your concern or were you just existing?

The fact that you're reading this book tells me that you were not just existing. The fact that you're reading this book tells me that there's something more that you're looking for in your life and I will tell you this, you can find it before that day comes.

One of my biggest fears is being on my deathbed and looking at my life and having regrets. Realizing all of the opportunities were in front of me, but I was too scared to take them. Too scared for different reasons. Maybe it was the security of what I currently had. Maybe it was the fear of disappointing someone. Maybe it was the fear of hurting someone else's feelings. Maybe it was the fear of being different from the environment which has trained me to be the same as everyone else.

Creativity is dying every single day. Individuality is dying right along with it. There is no time to be someone else. This is your opportunity, your one shot, your one life that you were granted by whoever... whatever. Your life, not theirs.

What are you going to do with that life? How are you going to make a change in your world today? You must not build a life that is going to be filled with regrets on your last day. I suppose you could start tomorrow. I suppose you can start next week. Next month. Next year.

We take life for granted as if tomorrow is guaranteed. Well, let me tell you that it's not guaranteed. If you have never had someone in your life pass away or the only people to pass away have been older people, I do not envy you. Experiencing the death of a friend, family member or a younger person in your life will change your perspective of how much time there is. I'll let you in on a little secret, there isn't much. This book is not meant to be grim, this book is meant to be a realistic reminder.

The purpose of this chapter is to help you understand the finite nature of life. To remind you of the finite nature of life. To help you embrace the finite nature of life. So is it possible that there is no tomorrow, next week, next month, or next year? What would you do if today was your last day? What would you change if you had 24 hours to live? Who would you say I'm sorry too? Who would you still try to impress? Who would you still try to be?

Maybe you're sitting here saying to yourself that you don't want to be anybody. You are original, you are yourself and you always have been. Perhaps you are. If you're the person reading this book who is absolutely original, then I'd like you to do an exercise.

I'd like you to think about all the things that you want to change in this world. All the things that you want to add to this world. I want you to think of every single goal that you have in this world. I want you to try to figure out WHY you've created those goals. If you were the last person on Earth would you still have those goals? Is it for you or is it to impress? Maybe this will help you to reflect. Maybe this book will help you see some of the things that you're doing are not even for you. They're not for your loved ones. They're for people you don't even know. They're for people you don't even see. Are you trying to get in better shape because of you? Because that's what you want for yourself? Or are you trying to get in better shape to impress them? Are you trying to get in better shape to impress the world around you? Are you trying to get the promotion for the status? Or are you doing these things to be prepared for life? Are you doing these things to provide value to the world? There are very different reasons to achieve a goal. What I want you to do is to think about the way that you would like to leave your mark on this world.

What are some of the things that you would love to be able to accomplish that bring value and change? I would say most people, particularly younger Americans, are focused on growth in a way which is so selfish that it is inevitably going to lead them to mediocrity.

Understand that you must search for yourself. Don't live your life for other people. You must live your life for you. Make the transition to be the most authentic and real version of who you were created to be.

There was a kid named J*** and this young man had a big dream. He wanted to grow up to become a United States Marine, serve his country and become one of the few and the proud. J*** was a skinny kid shaped like a plank. Small framed and as fragile as glass. A little white kid from Florida that couldn't have been more than 115 - 120 pounds. The idea people have of Marines is that they are big, strong, fast, and courageous. What most people don't know about United States Marines is that they don't start that way. That is who they become.

Despite the fears that people tried to impose on him, despite the negativity that people tried to bring to him, J*** was not going to stop following his dream of becoming a United States Marine. He would work out until his legs failed him and I'll tell you that it was the hardest time of his life. He would throw up often and go home sore. He would feel broken when he woke up in the morning but he didn't let that stop his courage. He didn't let that break his mind. He didn't let that slow him down. J*** was small but he had bravery in his heart. He knew in the depths of his mind he was made to do something great in this world.

He trained for months with grueling tenacity. He forced himself to get faster, stronger, and smarter. J*** developed an unbreakable mindset that was not going to allow him to fail. I worked with him as his recruiter and was on this journey with him.

I had the pleasure of meeting his mom, stepdad, brother, girlfriend, dog and all the people that mattered to him most. His family didn't initially support his dreams, but he was persistent with his vision. When they realized that his mind was made up and there was nothing that was going to stop him, they couldn't help but to admire the fire that so few of them had themselves so they had no choice but to begin supporting him.

He had every tool to succeed and become a man of character. He had every bit of confidence and courage needed to serve his country honorably as a United States Marine. The night before J*** was to ship to boot camp, he decided that he wanted to hang out with his girlfriend and say his final goodbyes. They hung out all day. They laid out by the pool, hugged and kissed and shared each other's breath. They told each other the stories of how life was going to be, describing the white picket fence and basking in the reality of their american dream. They thought about how they were going to get married and move around the Earth sharing fine foods, and visiting the wonders of the world. How they were finally going to be able to make a difference in their lives and break the cycle that was set for them. How they were finally going to be able to make a change that would inevitably change the course of their history. They were going to be free from the rule of adolescence which has trapped them for the past 18 years with a gripping strength.

After an amazing day, J*** decided to drive his girlfriend home, a three hour drive north up the coast of the great peninsula. It was late and it was dark, but J*** had the courage to do anything and he knew that he'd be fine. He would get her there safely because he was a Marine in training. He wasn't wrong. They arrived at her home and he walked her up the driveway. He held her hands in his and gave her that one final kiss goodbye. He tells her that the next time she sees him, he'll have accomplished something that very few Americans will ever be able to say they've accomplished and he was doing it for them. That next morning, I received a call from J***'s stepdad telling me that he wouldn't be able to ship to boot camp. His father proceeded to tell me J*** fell asleep behind the wheel, veered off the highway at almost 80 mph, and crashed into a camera pole on the side of I-95 which split his car in two and killed him on impact.

My heart sank into my stomach and I was unable to respond. The shock of what was just passed to me raised the hairs on my arms and I felt as if I was in a dream. The young man I had mentored, trained and cared deeply about was gone in the flash of a second. The journey he set out for ended like the power had been cut from his life.

What are the small lessons that teach you the finality of life? J*** would never serve as a United States Marine nor would he create his dream. J*** would never sleep in his bed or kiss his girlfriend again. J*** would never be able to build the life that he had planned with her. His chapter was done and life was forced to move on without him. J***'s story is not unique. These types of horrific accidents happen every day, all the time to the people that we love and care about. To our kids, our parents and our friends. It could happen to you.

This story is not to scare anyone or to be morbid. It's not meant to be grim or dark either. It is simply a reality of life that we quickly categorize as unique and only applies to someone else. The moral of the story is simply to be a reminder and an example that it doesn't matter what your dream is, it doesn't matter what your goals are, it doesn't matter what you want to do. Anything could happen at any time. The world does not wait for you and there is no time like the present. J*** didn't waste a minute of his life trying to achieve his goal or separate himself from the life that he had. Live your dreams. Act on your life as fast as you can with a fierce passion and a glowing heart. Start today because you don't know if there's going to be tomorrow. You never know when your chapter is going to end.

LESSON 3: THE PEOPLE AROUND US.

To gain the mindset necessary to achieve your goals you must believe in yourself above all else. However, believing in yourself sounds good when it's seen in a quote or used in marketing to attract buyers. When it's used to get you to motivate someone, they are just words. Understand this, believing in yourself is a really difficult thing to do 24 hours a day seven days a week. It's difficult because there are so many things around us that influence our belief in who we are.

Every single thing that negatively influences the belief we have in ourselves is created by another human being. You could wake up today and feel great about the way that you feel, the direction your life is going and the way you look. Yet, wake up tomorrow and be completely ashamed of how far you have yet to come, wondering why you even started and now be on the brink of letting it all go.

Every year that goes by, every day that goes by, every new app that's made to connect us, presents a new way to stifle the belief in ourselves. So many people are doing so many great things when you look through the lens of the internet. So many people who look better than you. So many people are living their dream. So many people travel the world. So many people are there to judge you. Watching, waiting and observing your every move.. The trolls. Question is, how do we separate peoples' opinions of us from the way we see ourselves?

How do we ignore the haters and the naysayers while still maintaining absolute truth and belief in our own abilities? We don't want to believe it but the truth is, the opinions of people do matter to us. It's very common to hear people say, "I don't care what people think about me" but I can't help but believe that is an untrue statement. I find that building a mindset to achieve victory, satisfaction, and self-actualization, takes an interesting type of social ignorance.

It's nice when the people around us believe in our dreams, goals, and ideas. It's nice when people support our small businesses, personal projects, and our hobbies. However, for every person that believes in you there are two or three people who can't wait to see you fail. They wait for the chance to say "I told you so." It's likely that they only want to see you fail because they lack the ability to start the journey that you have started. It scares them to be left behind in the world of mediocrity. It creates envy in their eyes and a tone of hatred in their kind encouraging phrases. The hardest part about believing in yourself is keeping that belief when few believe in you. When no one else believes in your product, dream or vision.

The main reason why people don't achieve their dreams is because they allow these haters and naysayers to shut them down from the inside. They allow them to plant the seeds of doubt. The secret to overcoming this is by being relentless in your dreams. By doing whatever it takes to accomplish your goal. But doing it without tangible results for the foreseeable future? That's where most fall short.

It's not going to be filled with supporters and people who care. People only care when they see it and until then you are often cast as dillusional. The road is lonely, dark and unforgiving. It doesn't happen overnight and there's no quick fix. There's no simple solution, there's no magic pill and there's no easy answers. It is pure will, grit, pain, suffering and absolute dedication to the future of your personal growth. Putting your back against the wall forcing you to grow. You must command your mindset to change. Demand it to do as you will.

Remember most of the major accomplishments ever achieved by humans were accomplished because there was no other option. They say that the people crazy enough to think that they could change the world usually do.

You never truly know what's going on in the eyes of the people around us. People have fake lives on social media. These people present themselves with the highlight reel, making their followers and friends think that they're doing better than they actually are. Depicting the illusion of security and hiding the emptiness and real image behind it. The self defense mechanism. A classic example of psychological deception. They implement the "fake it till you make it" strategy. The

"I'm an influencer" strategy, the "rent a Lamborghini" strategy. This can make you believe that you're behind in life. How can they be doing all these things and I'm just me? They are entitled to do what they want to do. The point is to not focus on the people around us.

When we focus on what the people around us have, do or think, it takes us off our track and stifles us in our own personal growth. Belief in oneself begins to diminish because we lack what everyone else seems to have and what they seem to be. But the truth is we have no idea what they do or do not have, nor should we care. We cannot allow people's success, illusion of success, or failures dictate and determine the trajectory of our own personal life.

Believing in yourself can be as simple as waking up and just deciding to believe in yourself. Just start the project, the journey, the program, the workout, the book, just start doing what it is that you need to do for you.

You must understand that not everybody in this life is going to be a success. Not everyone's going to be able to accomplish their dreams. Not because they are incapable, but because they can't release their mind from the social paralysis they have trapped themselves in. The majority live their entire lives and copy the copy. They turn into a clone of the clone and they regurgitate everything they see. When they have a moment of realization and come to the determination that it's all a lie, it's too late to make a change. They've wasted their entire life pretending to be someone else and there's no point in starting. Know this, It's never too late to start. The road will be long.

People that follow a trend because that's what's popular, spend every dollar they have on luxury products even though they can't save any money and carry the attitude of entitlement even though they have provided nothing to the world, will one day realize it's all been fake.

The point of this chapter is to help you realize you must be you. You cannot shape your life into a distorted version of a fake influencer. YOU have value to give to the world. YOU must find your vision, YOU must chase your goals and your aspirations.

What is the thing that makes you smile in the morning? You must find the one thing that only you could do and that if you didn't do, it probably wouldn't get done. Then you need to sacrifice every single bit of your time and effort to achieve the vision that only you can accomplish. The purpose for your life. All while ignoring the traps that are set for you by the people around you. Find yourself.

LESSON 4: MOTIVATION & DISCIPLINE

You must learn and understand the difference between discipline and motivation. See, discipline is the thing that separates the winners from the losers. Winners focus on winning while losers focus on winners. Discipline is the thing that will take you from having absolutely nothing to having anything you could've ever dreamed of in your life. Discipline does not come easily. Discipline is designed to be painful to reach. A slow process made from the chiseling of your soul. Refining yourself step by step and piece by piece. You show me an obese man, I will show you an undiscipline man. You show me a poor man, I will show you an undisciplined man. You show me a weak man, I will show you an undisciplined man. It is discipline that takes you from point A to point B.

Discipline is something that is created from the depths of a person's soul. You can't be gifted with it. You can't acquire it overnight or learn it in a class. It takes years of building, grinding, sacrifice and struggle. Whereas motivation can be given to you. Motivation is a gift. It can help you start the journey that you've been waiting to embark upon. It is the spark. Motivation can be brought to you in a speech. It could be brought to you in a video. It could be brought to you in a book. Motivation is something that is finite and lasts only as long as the day itself. It comes and goes like a pendulum but to be able to tackle long-term goals, one must build long lasting discipline to do so.

When you see people going to the gym on January 1st to get their "New Year, new me" body, they have decided it's time to make that change. The gyms are packed, the motivation is high, and everybody seems ready to tackle their objective. Be patient because when you wait a week or two all of a sudden, the gyms begin to empty. How about the alcoholic who loves to have a drink after work. One turns to 10, 10 turns to tomorrow a seemingly never ending cycle of personal destruction one sip at a time. They were motivated by something or someone and now they've decided to finally put it down because it's destroying the relationships of the people that they love, their kids and their job. The people in their life have finally convinced them to put the bottle down after crying and begging for them to hear their prayers. They have motivated this person and inspired this person to pick the love of their family over the alcohol.

But what happens the next time you have a hard day at work? The stress of that boss you can't stand always nibbling away at your soul. What happens the next time you lose your job? Facing the fear of homlessness and becoming a social pariah. What happens the next time your lover breaks up with you? Thinking about them being loved by another in a way you never could. What happens the next time, the next time, the next time, the next time.

See, motivation is temporary because motivation does not prepare you for the hard realities and crushing variables. The twisted humor of existence. Motivation does not prepare you for tough times that will test your willpower and make previous proclamations null and void. Mike Tyson has a saying, "Everyone's got a plan until they get punched in the face." Motivation is like taking a train around the world. The problem is, eventually the line will end. The track is not designed to cover long stretches of ocean. You will have to rely on a different vehicle to finish the journey. That vehicle oftentimes is a rowboat. Wood splintered, small, and frail. This boat represents discipline. A disciplined individual will get in the boat, tape up their hands, mount their oars and start rowing. They will begin to row, and they'll row and they'll row until they think they can't row anymore. They dig deep inside themselves and shift the limiter in their brain until they arrive at their destination because the discipline will not allow them to stop.

Discipline is created from habit. Discipline is second nature. We cannot be so blind as to assume that we have the discipline to achieve monumental goals if we don't even have the discipline to make our bed in the morning, exercise regularly, study, or even read. Now, maybe at this point you might realize that discipline is something that you need. The question now is how do you get it? It comes from a desire to want to win so badly that you allow nothing to get in your way. Usually that has to be followed by something else. Some type of shifting point in your life.

When I was 19 years old I was with a girl who I cared for deeply. I told my father my plan was to marry this woman and go off into the sunset. My dad in his wisdom warned me that I didn't know myself yet as a young man and I was sure to face major issues . I thought I did know myself. How would he know how I felt? I didn't take his advice because I knew best for myself, and I went ahead and I married her. Just as he said, things began to roll down hill. We fought and screamed at each other often. Sometimes things would get so bad we would break the house apart and lose respect for each other with the words we would vomit. She was bad, but I was worse. For the next four years I was verbally and mentally abusive to this young woman. I said and did things I will never be able to take back. I didn't treat her with respect. I did not treat her as an equal. In my eyes she couldn't understand the points I would make and through a continuous barrage of gaslighting sessions I eventually crushed her spirit.

The problem was, I was just a kid and I didn't know how to be with another person at that level because I didn't even know how to be with myself. I was impatient and just overall a terrible person to be around. Now this isn't to say we didn't have good times here and there because we did.

Although when it came down to it, all that got shadowed by our toxic relationship.

Ultimately, we came to a mutual agreement that the relationship would be over, that we would get divorced, and we would be young divorcees and that was that. We were going to go our separate ways. The next day she packed up the three boxes that she brought when she moved with me, put them into our car, drove back to our hometown four hours away, and I never saw her again. She wanted absolutely nothing to do with me. She ditched the car at my mothers house and erased all memory of who I was and I can't blame her for it.

For the next year I had malice in my heart. I was angry and I blamed her for the failure of our relationship. I blamed her for the destruction of my life. How could she do this to me? We had everything put together nicely. Solid place, nice cars, some money in the bank. Now all of a sudden, I was living in a one room barracks with nothing that I owned and everything I had from the house was thrown in the garbage or sold.

I was starting from ground zero. Months went by and I was depressed and sad. I couldn't figure out why she left me. I couldn't put the pieces together because I was so trapped in my viewpoint of the events that took place that I didn't see the reality of what I had done. In my head I really thought I was a good guy. Why did she leave me? I really thought I tried my best. Woe is me. The pity party has arrived.

I was lost in a delusion and my mind would not allow me to place the blame where it belonged.

Suddenly, I woke up one morning and I realized something very critical and it changed my life forever. I was a jealous, insecure loser. On my 23rd birthday I realized that the entire time that I had been with this girl, it was not her but me. I was the problem from the beginning. Had I taken my dad's advice and learned something about myself and the world before I tried to trap a woman's soul, I might have had the chance to grow up a bit and did it right the first time.

For some this may seem obvious. But it was more than that. The idea of who I grew to be was fake. The idea of my morality was an internal scam I ran on myself. I had no morality. When you're in something, when you're a part of it, when your perspective is on the inside, things can only be seen from one perspective per person. It takes an immense amount of maturity to see more than one angle and it takes a wise man to see them all. I blamed her and I talked bad about her because I couldn't face the fact that I was a bad choice. When I look back on this, as terrible as it is to say and as much damage as I probably caused that poor young woman, it was something that needed to happen for my own personal growth. It was at that moment I realized that I had to make a change in my life. That was my shift.

I still remember the day when I had this epiphany. It now seems so simple but as a young man it was not. I suppose that's the way the world works. They say that hindsight is 20/20. I wish foresight could be the same.

That next day I woke up and I realized that I didn't like who I was, and I didn't like the person that I was setting myself up to become. I didn't like where I was mentally, physically, emotionally, financially, or professionally. There was very little that I loved about myself at that point in my life. It was at this critical moment that I made a decision to make the most drastic change of my life up to this point. Shift.

The first thing I had to do was rebuild my mind because if I couldn't comprehend the world around me I would be trapped in a world meant for undesirables. Stage 2, I had to grow my body. If I didn't like the way I looked, I wouldn't like the way I felt. If I didn't like the way I felt, I wouldn't like the way I felt about others. If I didn't like the way I felt about others, how could I begin to provide value to people around me. I had to go internal and restructure my entire personality piece by piece.

I began to wake up at 4 o'clock in the morning every single day no matter if it was rain, sleet, or snow. I would walk to the gym and punish myself with long workouts and force my body to grow. I grew calluses on my hands and on my mind. I repeated this again and again and again until I didn't have to think about the process. After each workout I would then sit in the field next to where I lived and I would meditate.

I would think about who I wanted to be. How would my future kids see me? I would think about what type of person I wanted to become. I wanted to be a kind, honest, truthful, and hard-working individual. I thought about dedicating myself 100% to everything that I did. I did this to build a certain level of discipline in order to make and maintain this change. That level of discipline became a habit. That habit became a part of who I was. I began to be extremely effective at work, with my relationships and with my inner spirit. I was reconstructing over 20 years of bad habits and a weak mindset.

For the next 2 years I buried my face in books and I learned. I read everything I could about self-improvement, money and leadership. About what it was like to have a moral compass. I had to completely rebuild the individual that I was. As sad as that situation was, and as bad as I feel about how things were in that relationship, I'm grateful that it happened because for me that was one of my shifting points.

I'm sure that I will have many more shift points but I yet to see how they will be more influential than that one. So for that, I have to thank that girl. It's because of that relationship that I started the journey to become the man that I am today; respected by my colleagues, a loving husband to my wife, and a loving father to my son. A man of character, patience, and tact. Because of that situation in which I was so heartbroken and frustrated, it was enough to drive action. A change that will follow me until the day I die. It was a choice that was made that enough was enough and I needed to be who I was meant to be, not who I was taught to be.

People say "you are who you are" but I don't believe that. I believe you can be whoever you want to be. You can change today for the better or for the worse. You could wake up tomorrow and be a completely different person with a different mindset, different goals and in a different headspace that will allow you to achieve any dream you set your mind to.

There is no level of motivation that will allow you to make the changes that you need to make or build the dreams that you want to build. There is no amount of motivation that is going to set you up to deal with the level of pain and frustration that life will inevitably bring to you. It is only through pain, where we find our shift points and we must make a choice to evolve into the person that we are meant to be. Motivation is temporary. Discipline is who you are.

Shift.

LESSON5: HUNGER

In order to achieve a monumental goal in your life, in order to provide immense value to the world, you have to be hungry. When I say hungry, I don't mean hungry for money and I don't mean hungry to get the next promotion, I mean hungry to win at everything you do.

As I said before, the people who are crazy enough to think they can change the world usually can. You have to be obsessed with improving yourself. You have to be obsessed with changing, growing, developing and sharpening your mind. I heard a saying once that the lion on top of the mountain is not as hungry as a lion going up the mountain and I think that might actually be true.

See, a lot of people are born on top of the mountain and that's where they're lucky enough to stay in most cases. They don't have to fight for a dollar, a meal, a bed, a job or a degree, because somebody looked out for them in that way. The way that many people do not have. Many of us have to find our own path and you have to find your path too. On your path, you have to maintain your hunger and to increase your appetite as you grow. There will be mistakes and missteps along the way but you must keep climbing.

I recommend adopting the big picture mindset because it's not always about how you get there, it's just the fact that you got there. What is the big picture? What is the goal and how bad do you want it?

Visualize the target. What is the objective? What is your mission? Figure it out, see it, visualize it, feel it and embrace it. How does it taste, how does it smell, how does it feel, what does it look like?

Use your senses to envision the future that you want for yourself. Once you get a good visual picture of what that looks like, filling in the gaps between now and then becomes the easy part. First, you have to know what you want. This dream fades if you get overwhelmed by the distance that you must climb in order to achieve it.

Some people are lucky enough to start at higher levels of the mountain. Some of us have to start underground. One of the biggest issues that I see people struggling with is that a challenge, obstacle or goal will be so far, it will seem so distant that people don't even bother trying at all.

You have to eradicate that type of thinking from your brain and do whatever it takes to achieve your goal. Be unrealistic in your hunger. You need to want it, you need to dream about it, you need to pretend to already have it. You need to adopt a zero fail mentality. I have to thank the United States Marine Corps for fine tuning my zero fail mentality but that's not where it began.

Many people grow up the way I grew up. With absolutely nothing. I know what it's like to be poor beyond poor. I know what it's like to be five years old, taking two buses and a trolley to get to school by yourself and paying the $3 it cost, in pennies. The embarrassment as you clog the rectangular machine… Poverty was a way of life for me. It was not something that I adopted, it was something I was accustomed to. I didn't fall into it. I was the definition of it. It was something that I was born with and something that defined who I was as a child.

When I say poverty I don't just mean financial poverty, I mean mental poverty. Trapped in a world of ignorance and stupidity. The people in my community didn't want better for themselves. Trash littered the streets as it did their minds. People who do not want to achieve more for themselves surrounded me in droves. People waiting for a government check, capable of working for a living but choosing not too. Food stamps were a bargaining chip, being sold outside the grocery store for cash to buy drugs. Someone would have $400 in food stamps and trade them for $200 in cash. Business was good I suppose.

I remember looking at all the other kids at school who would bring lunches with all kinds of snacks from home. Juice boxes, cookies, sandwiches, goldfish all packed with care and attention to detail. Perfectly portioned to feed the little stomachs of which they were prepared for.

I remember in first grade a kid threw out an entire pack of cookies after eating just one. I was so disturbed, I snuck my way over to the trash can so as to not draw attention to myself. I slid close to the receptacle and reached into it without looking down. I was as smooth as a ninja. I grabbed the cookies and couldn't wait to dig into the chocolate chip flavor. Never did get the chance. I got caught eating them out of the trashcan by the teacher.

I could go on for hours about the different things I've been through in my childhood. They have given me the mentality that I have today but that's not the point of this book. The reason I tell you this story is because you have to think about where your hunger came from or will come from.

It doesn't matter if you're starting at the top of daddy's mountain. If daddy is the one who is taking care of everything for you and you're reading this book it's because you recognize that it's not your success. It's OK to be gifted a lifestyle that is better than some of us. It's not a bad thing to have people that care about you but it doesn't mean that you're exempt from earning your own mental and physical growth. You are not exempt from developing your own vision and your own value for this world.

For those of you reading this book, you need to find that thing that makes you hungry and you need to think about it. You must reflect on the past in order to get hungry for the future. Once you find that thing that makes you hungry, let that be the engine that drives you as far away from that potential reality as possible.

Dig deep inside yourself and develop a hunger to win at everything you do. Win at brushing your teeth. Win at making your bed. Beat yourself at everything you did yesterday, today. Find the thing that makes you hungry and never let go of it. Don't cram it away. Don't try to swallow your trauma. Don't bottle it, close it and secure it in the back of the closet. Take it out, sit it right in front of you, look at it and beat the hell out of it.

Eat it.

LESSON 6: BACK AGAINST THE WALL

You have to be willing to put your back against the wall. You have to be willing to have no way out. If you're willing to put yourself in an uncomfortable position, there's almost a 100% guarantee that you are going to achieve your goal. One of the main things that stops people from making decisions that will change their lives for the better is comfortability.

Being comfortable is another way of saying that you're scared. You're scared of the unknown, you're scared of what's on the other side, you're scared of the path that you can't see. You're scared about what happens if you make the wrong choice and I'm gonna tell you something, you will make wrong choices from time to time, but the wrong move is better than no move.

A baby chicken must break through its own shell in order to find the strength necessary to survive in life. In order to gain the animalistic instinct that it needs for everyday survival, it must break through its own birth environment. The right of passage. If somebody or something were to break the shell for the chicken, that chicken will die within weeks. We are very similar except our physical body will not die. Our minds will.

Who have you been letting break your shell? Who's been giving you the answers, solving your problems, paying your rent or picking up the slack for you? Who is the person that you lean on every time you mess up your life? Who is the person you fall back on time and time again. Is it your mom, your dad, your brothers, your sisters? Is it your girlfriend, your boyfriend, your husband, or your wife? Who is it? You have to stop using this person as a crutch.

If you picked up this book it's because you're ready to change your mindset to accomplish whatever mission you set out for yourself. You have to be willing to make decisions that are going to make you uncomfortable and scared. These types of decisions are very similar to getting on a roller coaster.

You stand in line for hours and as you wait there you get closer and closer to the front of the ride and it's gigantic. It's making you extremely nervous as you approach the gate. Finally, after an hour of

79

waiting patiently, for something that you've been dreading, it's your time to get on the roller coaster. Your heart is beating and you're ready to turn around and go the other direction. Against your better judgment, too scared of inconveniencing everyone behind you, you get on the roller coaster anyway. The attendant puts down the guard and locks you in place. All of a sudden you hear the air brakes go off and that roller coaster climbs 400 feet and shoots you directly to the ground! It's going extremely fast, it's got a lot of twists and turns, and it's scaring the crap out of you, but your adrenaline is rushing and you feel excitement not fear. What happens when you get off the roller coaster?

How do you feel at this moment? Nine times out of 10, you're probably ready to get back on the roller coaster and do it again because it was exciting, because it was something that got your blood going, it was something that woke you up! This might seem like a weird analogy, but life is exactly the same way. You need to find something that wakes you up and snaps you out of the coma that life and social media has put you in.

Sometimes when things are unknown and there is no clear path, it allows you to take control of your destiny and build your foundation the way you want it to be. You don't allow someone else to build your story for you, an entity to put a system around your life or an institution to lock away your creativity. If you want to accomplish massive goals and big dreams, you cannot allow an institution or culture to put barriers on your soul and systematically control your life.

Ask yourself this question, when you get to the top of whatever ladder you're currently climbing ,will you like the view from the top? What do you see for yourself there? Is it everything that you imagined it would be? It's not uncommon to get caught in this type of trap.

I lived in a world that was designed for me. A rulebook was put in place. Guidelines. Someone told me where to go, when to go, and how to go. It was a comfortable life, good living, and provided me with a sense of value for a time. One day I had to ask myself…is this it? Is this the culmination of my life? When I retire from this job will I be satisfied with the value that I've provided? At almost 40 years old, I would hang up that hat for the last time, halfway through my life and start something new. How tired would I be? Would I be willing to start a new journey?

Ever since I was a young kid I always had a vision of changing the world somehow. Kids are funny in that way. They all have a dream, they all have a vision, they all have a goal and they all have a person that they want to be. A firefighter, a police officer, an astronaut, a performer.

Something changes somewhere along the line. I'm not sure where it happens. I'm not sure how it happens, but something changes. We make a weird transition from doing what we want to do, to doing what we have to do. Kids are fearless and do what they want when they want. They will give you the shirt off their back. They're pure and energetic and have fun with everything that they do.

At what point in life does that go away? At what point in life do we let things get so out of hand, so frustrating, so consuming that we are no longer that same energetic, inspired, fun loving kid that we once were?

When did we become selfish and scared? How is it that we can digress as we progress? This transition happens to us all because we're very similar in many ways.

Some of us recognized the transition and we don't like the way it feels. So what do we do? We find a way to go back to living life on our own terms. That's what I had to do and that's what you need to do. I had to put my back against the wall and lose everything in order to grow. Another strength that I acquired throughout my life of growing up underground beneath the mountain is that I'm able to adapt.

When I was young, we used to end up homeless frequently. My mom would pick me up from school and we would take the bus and trolley back to the apartment where we would come across the sheriffs inside of our home. They would be taking all the things out and putting them on the sidewalk. They would clear the apartment for the owner. It was someone else's home now. Who needed the home more than me? Too young to realize it didn't matter and too young to realize that 4 months behind on rent tends to do that.

She would shamelessly tell me to grab a bag and put everything that I could fit into it because we weren't coming back. I would grab my favorite toys off the curb and place them into my bag. My mom would recommend the clothes. It was really the embarrassment I learned to get used to. That type of shame will scar a person without leaving any marks. Off we would go to find a couch to crash.

This happened more than once. The lesson that I learned each time it happened, was that we got better. I got better. I got stronger and less attached to the things that never mattered. Here I am 20+ years later, realizing that those lessons I learned when I was a young kid were preparing for the moments where I again needed to put my back against the wall.

As this new chapter ends, I realize the amount of growth that has occurred during this period of time, 11 1/2 years worth, has come to an end in this arena. The world moves on without us. My focus must shift. Shift.

There's more that I have to give the world, and I know that there's more that you can give the world too. So even though you're nervous and even though you're scared, take the lessons from me and know that it's ok if you have to pack your bag, reset your life and start over from scratch.

Know that it's OK because you will get stronger, you will get better, you will grow and develop and you will win. You have no choice but to win. That's the point you must understand. No one told you that life was going to be fair, no one said that life was going to be easy, and if they did, they would have lied to you. If they did lie to you, where are they now and how come you are looking for answers in this life alone. That, in and of itself, is a lesson. Talk is cheap. Quotes are cool when they're on a shirt, but this is real life, your one life, your only life. Keep climbing.

LESSON 7: IMPOSTER

I want you to think of the most average person you've ever met in your life. This person doesn't do the extra work, they don't work the extra hours, they don't go the extra mile, they are just there. They're not good, they're not bad, they just are. This person is the most average person in your memory bank. What I want you to realize is that half the people in the world are worse than them. Half the people in the world work less, have less passion, have less drive and yield less results.

The world can be summed up in what I call the Diamond Diagram. 10% of the world's population are in the pinnacle of this chart. They are the sharpest, smartest and most qualified individuals. The next 15% of the world falls in the above average category. The hard-working people dedicated to what they do and willing to go the extra mile. 50% of the world are average people. People that just live in a world of breathing, working and dying. They don't even realize that they're just living, they don't even realize that there's more to life than the things that they're currently involved in. They wait to get off work as early as they can, they contribute as little as possible and fall through the cracks. The 15% below them are the lost people. The delusional people. The people that contribute nothing to society, but they take nothing from society. The bottom 10% are the criminals, the crooks, the welfare scammers.

These people will take the shirt off your back and the food out of your child's mouth just to get what they want for that day without a thought to who it hurts or what others may feel. These people have little to no moral compass and absolutely zero ambition to create anything of substantial value and provide nothing to the world around them. As you can see, there's a lot of space in between the top and the bottom of this Diamond Diagram. This is where the majority of people fall in. In order to build a winning mindset, you have to have an insatiable desire to reach the top 10%.

Now, this is not a financial graph. This graph indicates the level of a person's inner character. You could be a billionaire and be at the bottom 10% of this chart. You could be a homeless man with absolutely nothing and be at the top 10%. This chart simply indicates one's ABILITY to create the mindset necessary to make everlasting change in the world around them. Our society promotes rappers, gangsters, social media influencers, scammers, and frauds as artists and creatives. However, it's a smoke screen. What they're doing is destroying the minds of the culture in which they claim to represent.

In the history of the world there has never been such a vile cancer to spoil the minds of our youth. People are growing up faster and dumber than ever. Waiting for the next puppet master to pull the strings while the entire time thinking that they are the ones in control. The desire to create an everlasting difference in the world is almost completely eradicated. "How can we get as much as possible and do as little as possible?"

You have to be willing to separate yourself from the social norms and recognize that feelings and opinions do not coincide with real change, real results or reality. You have to be willing to accept facts for facts, and understand that in order to reach the top 10% it takes knowing oneself, being authentic to oneself and escaping the prison in which media outlets and the social network have locked the majority of us in.

There are so many people in the world that do what you want to do.

Whatever dream it is that you have, whatever goal it is that you have, whatever value you want to provide, someone else is already doing it. And they're probably doing it effectively and that's OK. That doesn't mean that they're creating the most value. You have to understand that there's enough space in this epidermal arena for more than one professional. There's an audience for you.

You cannot allow your opinion of one's success to prevent you from excelling in your own vision. With all the people in the world that seem to be doing so many great things, creating so many awesome businesses, so many amazing dreams and helping so many people, you have to have the confidence to know that the majority of them are not genuine.

They'll preach spirituality then ask about the revenue gained from the webinar. They'll teach you how to treat your spouse or other people in your life but then treat the people around them like slaves. They'll be your life coach and guide you to success, while they themselves can't even manage their own struggles and take their own advice. There is a space for you to be authentic in what you do and provide an everlasting change in the niche that you want to build. There is space, because very few people are able to do both.

You have to understand that if you are passionate about what you want to do in life and you understand the system in which it takes place, you are capable of creating something amazing in that sphere. Don't be intimidated by the noise of the world. You are not an imposter.

Do you have an opportunity in front of you? Learn as much as you can about the area you want to influence. Take the time to build a system that provides real change to the people you want to help. Once ready, step into that space with confidence knowing that as time goes on you will get better, sharper, smarter, more effective, and more efficient in your craft. You are the top 10% and understand there is no shortcut. You must understand that there is no easy way.

You must believe in yourself.

You are not an imposter.

LESSON 8: FLIP THE SWITCH

I hope the reader of this book understands that they have immense power. A power that can only be described as unbelievable. If you are sad, you have the power to change your mind right now and be happy! Put a smile on your face, stand up, take a deep breath and scream at the top of your lungs that you are happy! All of a sudden guess what happens?
You change your mindset.

If you are broke, you have the power right now at this very instant to make the decision to save your money and invest in something better than what you currently spend it on. You have the power to cut your spending, to cut your purchases, to focus on a different financial goal right now. If you are out of shape, you have the power to stand up, put your shoes on and go for a walk or a run and begin a transformation of your body and your mind. You can do that right now, in this very minute, there's nothing stopping you.

You have the power inside of you to flip the switch that changes the direction of your life. I don't care how far down the metaphoric hole of life you've traveled. I don't care how dark it seems. I don't care if nobody is near you. I don't care if no one is willing to help. I don't care if you were lost for the entirety of your life and now you have nothing left but a shell of the man or woman you once were. You have the power to make a change and move in the opposite direction of which you are currently moving.

Visualize the light switch on the wall… that is you! You are the light switch. Right now your light might be on or it might be off. Just as easily as you could walk over to that light switch and flip it the other way you can do the same thing with your mindset.

Doing this could change the direction and the course of history for you. I've always been a big picture kind of guy and I'll let you know that if you decide to flip that light switch, that's called the big picture. The big picture is changing your destination. Everything else will fall in between. When you decide to flip that switch now, all of a sudden, you will stop hanging out with the people that are bringing you down. You will stop involving yourself in the activities that are leading you in the wrong direction. When you flip the switch, the next time someone calls you and asks you to come out and spend your money at the bar, you will stay in the house and pick up a book. You will build your mind instead.

Everything in between will fall into place, but you have to make a decision to flip the switch. That's all it comes down to. Making the decision to flip the switch. The question is, how tired are you of traveling the direction that you're going? Because if you're not ready to flip the switch, then it's not going to happen.

You have to be ready to change your mindset in order for your mindset to change. Easier said than done.

Never forget, just as easily as you could flip the switch on, you can switch it right back off.

Are you tired of being sick and tired? Are you tired of being broke? Are you tired of being out of shape? Are you tired of living a random existence that is not what you visualized for yourself? You can be anyone you want to be, do anything you want to do, have any career you want to have, you just have to be willing to put in the work.

I know that sounds simple and people will read this and say it's not that easy, but the truth is, it is that easy. You just have to start working toward it one small step at a time. Eventually you'll arrive at your destination. This might require you to learn something new. In the frustration of learning something new, it often can be just enough to freeze someone's growth.

Let's take a small example of learning an instrument. A lot of people wish that they were musical. They say "oh man, I wish I learned how to play the piano, I wish I had learned how to play the guitar." But wishing it's not enough. Just go do it. Buy the piano, buy the guitar, and go do it. We have an abundance of information in front of us.

Most people in this world have a computer in their pocket 24/7. A small universe with endless information you can use to access anything that you want to learn, read anything that you want to read, build anything that you want to build, from any location around the world in the palm of your hand. There are hundreds of thousands of hours of "how to learn the piano" videos on YouTube and Google. There is absolutely nothing stopping you from doing it except for the frustration of learning something new.

Everyone wants to have fun immediately and this is where things begin to get complicated. This is the point that separates the average, middle section of our Diamond Diagram to the top 10%. It's the people who are willing to deal with the frustrations, the weird sounds, the embarrassment and the angry neighbors, who ultimately become successful at learning this new instrument. Most people will pick it up for a day or a week, they don't like the results, and they're not having fun, so they stop. This might seem like just one example of learning something new, but this translates into so many things in life. This translates into businesses, your career and your relationships.

People want the results and they want them now. We've been conditioned to have anything we want at the snap of a finger so when we can't get what we want, immediately, we're turned off by it. We live in a world of instant gratification. We move on from it because our attention spans are so small, we're unwilling to do the work for the things that we claim to want.

To learn what you want to do, you must be OK with sucking. You must be OK with not being good for a while. You must be OK with being frustrated because eventually things will begin to click. Learning, growing, and building is exponential. In the beginning, it is extremely slow and it seems like it's going nowhere but as you get better, you get better faster.

You're able to connect the dots. You're able to understand the craft and learn at a quicker pace. New projects take less time. New songs take less time. New business acquisitions take less time to acquire. New deals take less time to close. It's not because it got easier, it's because you got better. The imposter is the one who pretends to know, but is unwilling to put in the work. You are not an imposter. You're the top 10%. Grow, build, repeat. Flip.

LESSON 9: LESSONS OF OTHERS

The weird thing about humanity is that we often need to learn lessons the hard way. We could see the visual proof, we could hear the stories, we could see it with our own eyes, but if it doesn't have a direct effect on us, we often have a weird belief that it's not going to happen to us.

I will let you know, that's simply not the case. Earlier in this book I alluded to a story about a past relationship that I had. Even though I was told that it would probably be a mistake due to my own immaturity, I had to learn that lesson the hard way. You only know what you know.

One of the biggest things that I wish I could do is verbalize how imperative it is to take the lessons from other people and utilize them in your own existence. You don't have to go through the same struggles that other people have gone through. They say that if you study your history you can learn lessons in order to not repeat the mistakes of the past. However, you have to be willing to open your eyes and observe what happened and why it happened. Then apply them in your own steps and avoid the same pitfalls.

A lot of times we don't take an opportunity to do a real analysis of the what and the why. We see the "what". We see what happened and we assume why it happened, but we don't put much thought into the "why." "Things will be different for me."

When I was a young Marine, I used to love driving fast. I never had any money growing up and my family didn't own a car so when I finally had a few dollars in my pocket, the first place I went was a dealership and I bought my first car. It was a 2008 Honda Civic SI and I loved that car. The shape of the windshield with a short hood. It was sporty and aggressive with a six speed manual transmission that I didn't know how to drive and a 2.0 liter engine with a V8 attitude. I loved fixing it up, building it up and increasing its horsepower way above what it was capable of producing.

Ultimately it led me to a community of people that loved the same things and I joined a small car group. I was a rebel and a respected member of the team. I was justified and overconfident. Over the span of the next two years I would receive almost 30 speeding violations, be arrested on two separate occasions for street racing and would pay over $15,000 in court fines and fees. I almost lost my career as a United States Marine because of my inability to stop speeding. No amount of paperwork from my job, corrections from my sergeants, court fees or any amount of ass chewing, would stop me from getting behind the wheel and thinking that I was invincible. I was different. I wasn't going to die, I wasn't going to crash, I was going to be just fine.

In that car club I met a best friend named C**** who was a great hard-working kid. His dad was a very successful businessman in Hawaii that owned many different establishments around the island. C**** grew up knowing that he would be able to take over his father's company, be successful, and live a good life climbing his daddy's mountain.

We grew very close, and we developed a relationship that was closer than friendship, more like brothers. We went everywhere together and did everything together. We enjoyed the world in a way that would make any kid in his early 20's jealous. I looked up to him, and he looked up to me. We lived life on our terms and did what we wanted to do despite the warnings from the people that loved us. C**** wanted to branch off away from his father and grow his own empire and his own lifestyle. He understood the need to climb the mountain for himself and gain his own right of passage. I always admired him for that.

He and his new wife, who was pregnant with his first child, asked if they could move into my home with me and my wife at the time. Without hesitation, I said yes and the four of us grew even closer. During this time there were multiple attempts to try to change the behaviors in which both he and I had. Living life in a way that was both irresponsible and exciting. Fast lane.

One night he asked me to come out with him to check out his new car, a 1998 Honda Civic hatchback. "Do you want to go for a ride with me? Come out and cruise?" That night I had duty and I had to go stay at the barracks and stand guard so I told him I couldn't go along. I got my things together and went off to work and I stood my post as a Marine does.

About four hours into my duty at about 9 PM I get a call from a friend of ours with some alarming news. I was told that C**** was in a very serious car accident and that the ambulance was going to be taking him to Queens Medical Center in Downtown Waikiki. The first Marine I saw, I directed her to put the uniform on and take my post. I jumped in my car and I drove as fast as I could to Queens Medical Center, swerving in and out of traffic, taking shoulder lanes and pushing that honda to the redline. I made it to the hospital well before the ambulance arrived and when it finally did, they took him out, rolled him into the doors and what I saw shocked me to my core. I looked at this man as he was unconscious and unable to breathe with his arms and legs completely shattered. He was in pieces. His body was swollen and it was like the scene of a movie. People were running around screaming "code blue" this and "85 milligrams" that.

For the next nine hours the medical staff did everything they could to keep C**** alive. There weren't enough nurses and doctors on duty to treat him so his father and I were in the emergency room working tirelessly with the staff pumping the oxygen bag to try to get his lungs to open. Time after time we would have to flip him on his side as his lungs would drain fluid liter by liter. We would pump for what seemed like hours until our hands would cramp and then we would switch. "Ready to flip" we would grab the sheet from under his body and pull him to our stomachs as the yellow bile would squirt out of the mouthpiece jammed into his throat. "Drop!", the cycle would repeat.

The rest of the night was a blur but what I do know is I stayed in the hospital for at least the next 2 1/2 days. Finally C**** was in stable condition but completely unconscious. His injuries were extremely severe. He had completely shattered his pelvis, shattered both his legs and both his arms and at the time the extent of his injuries to his brain was undetermined since he was in a coma.

As good of a driver as C**** was, nothing can protect you from the randomness of life. When the paramedics found him and the other passenger, the car looked like a bunched up ball of tinfoil. They couldn't identify who the driver was and the engine was sitting on top of C****. It took almost an hour for the paramedics and fire department to get them out of the vehicle. C**** was unstoppable, he was a warrior. But even C**** was human.

He battled heart failure, liver failure, kidney failure, fat embolisms and so on. I would sit in the hospital day after day watching the ecmo machines pump oxygenated blood cells into his heart. I would listen as the dialysis machine would filter his kidneys and rid his body of infection. As a miracle would have it, he began to recover very slowly month after month. He eventually woke up from his coma and after a few days he was able to see and speak slowly. It actually seemed like he would get better and perhaps even have a somewhat full recovery. His daughter was born in the same hospital he was in and he had the chance to hold his baby for the first time. We didn't know it would be the only time.

One day during a visit he asked me to look at his new watch. His words were "Check out my OG watch, man." He was visualizing something on his wrist. I had to tell him there was nothing there. I came to find out later that day he had another infection and this one was spreading quickly to his brain. The infection started in his legs so his father had to make the hard choice to have them cut off. Despite their best efforts the infection wouldn't stop. C**** died that same day. Just like that he was gone.

I don't tell you this story to depress you, I tell you the story because that was the hard lesson that I needed to learn for me to change my habits. There was nothing that anyone could tell me that would stop me from driving the way that I did. But this event scared me straight. Had C**** took the advice that his father gave him, had I taken the advice that my peers and my superiors had given me, had I been able to convince C**** to take the same path that I could have, it's possible he would still be alive today.

Sometimes in life you have to learn lessons the hard way. This lesson unfortunately cost C**** his life. Maybe it's a relationship that's abusive. Maybe it's a relationship with drugs or alcohol. Maybe it's the lack of following a dream. You could take the story and move it 1000 different directions, but the point is you must not learn every lesson the hard way. Sometimes you just have to have the discipline to listen. Some advice is good advice. Sometimes you have to take the lessons of others.

LESSON 10: BUILD YOUR PLAN AND EXECUTE

It's time to figure out what you want. It's time for you to build your plan. Build your goals, write them down and follow through with them. It doesn't matter how crazy they may be or how obscure they may seem, you have to start the process.

First thing you should do is start your successful habits. Every day you should wake up before 5 AM and take the time necessary to get your thoughts together. If you start work at 5 AM then wake up at 3 AM. If you start work at 10 AM then wake up at 5 AM. The point of this is to get your energy for the day, get your thoughts together and take this time for yourself. This is the type of meditation that's going to allow you to start on the right foot.

A lot of people like to wake up right before they have to leave for work and I'll tell you, starting your day like this will make you tired, exhausted, have zero energy and you'll be less productive than you could be.

The next thing you need to set for yourself is a workout regimen, if you don't already have one. You need to set a time for yourself to work out five times a week. I recommend you do it in the morning, however if your schedule does not allow it, then do it in the afternoons or the evenings, but either way it needs to happen every single day. Follow this with a warm shower to get your body and your soul clean and ready for the day's events. Dress yourself in a way that will allow you to feel confident and ready to handle business. The way that you feel after a solid morning routine is unmatched. It makes you feel alive and ready to crush your objectives. You must develop the foundation for self-discipline.

Now, get yourself a composition book where you can write down all your goals and all of your dreams one by one. Identify exactly what it is that you want and put timelines in there for when you'd like to have them accomplished. Keep this book close to you and use it to write down anything and everything that comes to mind. You never know when a thought will come.

Take a vested interest in everything that goes on throughout your day. If you're at work and you have a project that your boss asks you to complete, put 100% of your energy and focus into that. If you start your own project, if you start your own business, put 100% of yourself into that. The focus here is attention to detail in everything that you do. From the way you make your money all the way down to the way you brush your teeth.

Only use your social media for business purposes. Don't use it to watch endless videos with mindless content. We are all subject to this at one point or another. You sit there and you realize it's a gigantic waste of time. If you put the phone down, if you took the PlayStation controller out of your hand, if you turned the TV off, you'd realize that you were just sitting there doing absolutely nothing and that it was a period of time in which you were standing completely still.

Now, I'm not saying to get rid of any type of downtime, I'm talking about the endless hours of just sitting there wasting your life with the little bit of time that you actually do have outside of your professional obligations.

Every day should be an opportunity for you to be as productive as possible. Doing something that creates value for your own personal life and subsequently creates value for the people around you. Every day you should be doing something that's going to get you closer to your goal.

You know, I have a saying; if you're not getting better you're getting worse and I believe in that because there's no in-between. If you're not using your time to get mentally physically, spiritually, or professionally better, you're getting worse. If you're using the time to hang out at the bars, party and sit there doing absolutely nothing but stare at screens then you are getting worse. The reason why you're getting worse is because every second that passes you are getting one second older.

Time is the one thing you will never get back, so it is extremely important for you to start building the mindset of a champion. Once you have an idea of what you want to do and your plan is built, take action on it. Don't be an imposter. Don't be a time bandit. Don't waste your life. What I'm asking you to do is take an opportunity to learn from the lessons that you've seen before.

Flip the switch and guide yourself toward the lifestyle that you want to have. Just make the choice to change. I hope that you found value in this book. It's short, but hopefully impactful. I wanted to give you an idea of what goes through my mind daily and why it has allowed me to excel in the small details of my life.

I'm not a millionaire. However, in my mind I know that I'm destined for something great and I want to share that message with you because I think that if people adopted this mindset the world would be a better place. Flip. Shift. Start…

Follow me on instagram @dutton_mindset

Visit Duttonmindset.com to learn more.

Thank you.

Made in the USA
Las Vegas, NV
10 July 2024

92108455R00075